Wildlife of
Cactus and Canyon Country

Written and illustrated by Marj Dunmire

Contents

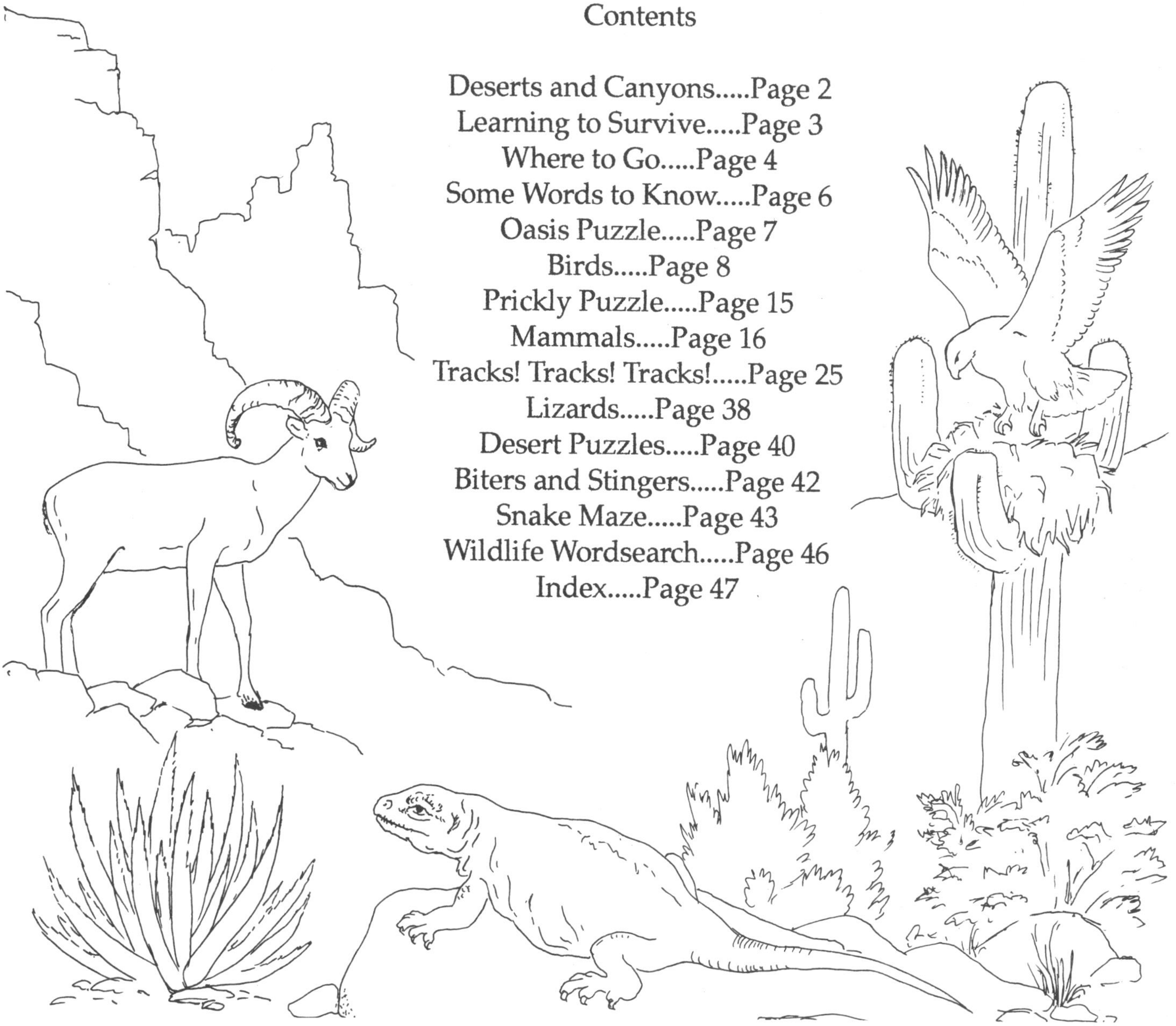

My thanks to all the people who have made this book possible: to my sons, Glenn who accompanied me on some trips to the desert, and Peter who helped with editing and typesetting; to many others who offered helpful information, read manuscript, and encouraged me along the way.

Design by Pegasus Graphics
ISBN: 0-942559-05-3
Printed on Recycled Paper

Published by:
D & L Distribution,
PO Box 72,
Cahone, CO 81320

DESERTS

It's dry. It's hot.
But barren it's not.
A land of contrast, a land of Light,
And strange creatures out at night.
Many things you'll find alive,
But how in the world do they survive?
Rain falls very seldom and doesn't last.
The sun comes along and dries it fast.
After a rain the desert floor
Is covered all over with flowers galore.
With a huff and a puff the wind blows about.
When night comes along, animals come out
To look for their food while the air is cool,
And perhaps take a drink at some lingering pool.
It's fun to explore this curious land,
To run about and play in the sand.
But do be careful and watch where you tread.
Here life is so fragile, just held by a thread.
Look and take pictures but please let things be,
For others to come, enjoy, and see.

teddybear cholla

CANYONS

Across the desert broad and wide
Here and there rise mountains high.
Rivers wind their way along
Carving great canyons deep and long.
Some are narrow with steep rock walls,
Little side canyons, and waterfalls.
Others shelter trees, animals, and flowers,
Especially after desert showers.

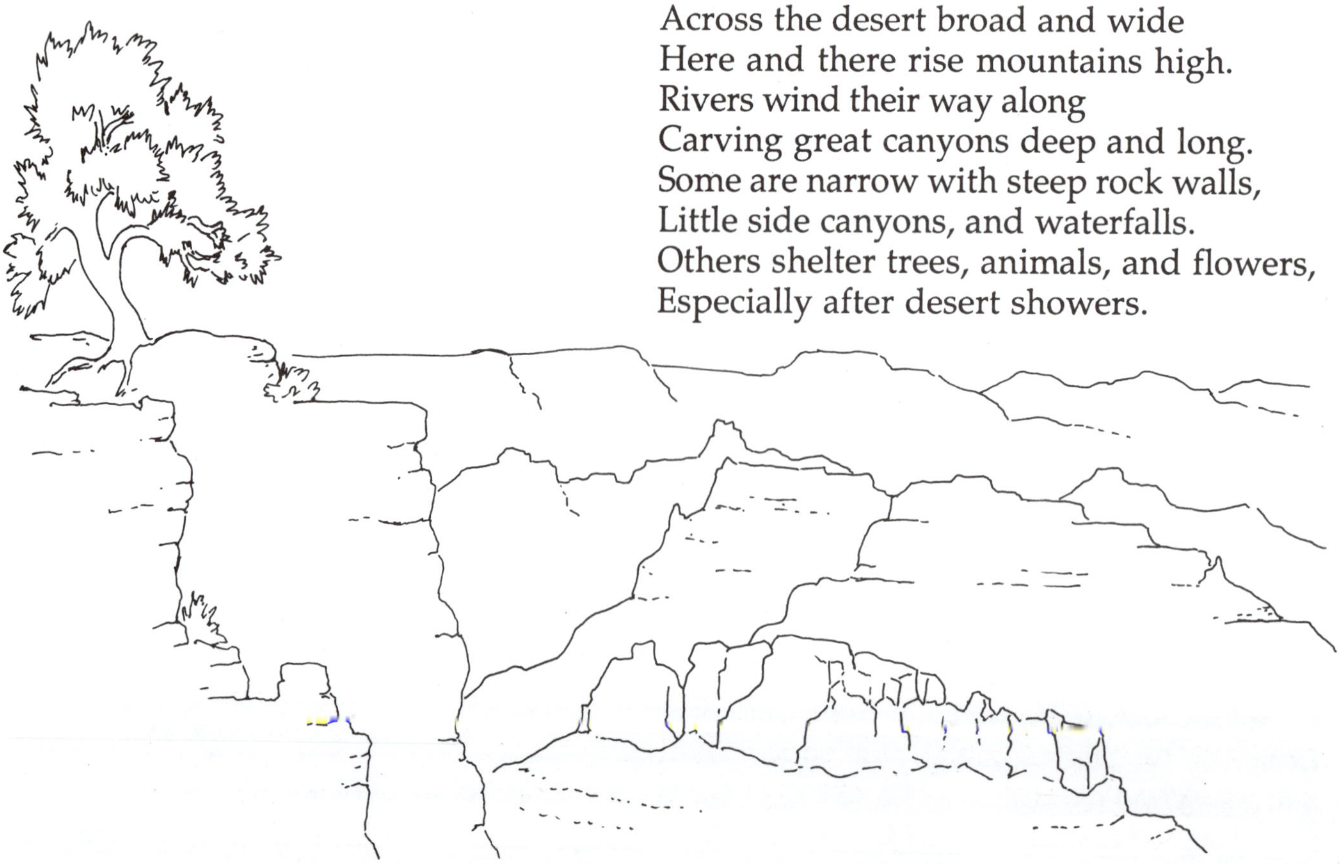

Learning to Survive —A Puzzle

beavertail cactus

1. — — — — —
2. — — — — — — —
3. — — — — —
4. — — — — — —
5. — — — — —
6. — — — — — —
7. — — — — —
8. — — — — — — —
9. — — — —
10. — — — — — — — —
11. — — — — —

Use the sentence clues below to find the words to this puzzle. The outlined word is the key to wildlife survival.

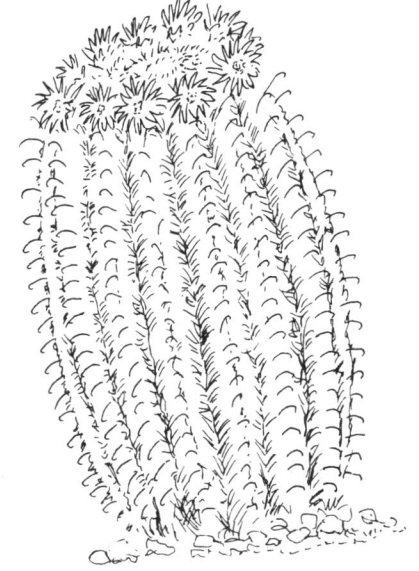

barrel cactus

1. Some plants have a _ _ _ _ coating to cut down on loss of moisture.
2. Others have seeds that stay in the ground asleep, or are _ _ _ _ _ _ _ until it rains.
3. Often stems and leaves are covered with fine _ _ _ _ _ that give shade.
4. Sharp _ _ _ _ _ _ on cactus keep many animals from eating them.
5. Plants grow far apart so their _ _ _ _ _ can spread out and soak up more rain.
6. _ _ _ _ _ _ and flowers grow on some plants only when there is enough rain or moisture.
7. Saguaro and barrel cactus have thick stems that can expand and _ _ _ _ _ water.
8. A rabbit's big ears pick up sound and also help cool by _ _ _ _ _ _ _ _ _ heat.
9. Some animals never drink water. They get moisture from the _ _ _ _ they eat.
10. Other animals stay cool and save moisture by coming out at night. They are _ _ _ _ _ _ _ _ _.
11. Some animals _ _ _ _ _ during the driest times. This is called estivation.

Answer on page 45

Where to Go

The map of southwestern U.S. on the next page has broad outlines (:※:) of the main desert areas. Boundaries are not sharply defined and in some places they overlap. How do you know where one ends or begins? There are some things called indicator species, that tell us when we are in a certain desert. Here is what to look for in each one.

Great Basin Desert is the highest and farthest north. It is the coldest and does not have the large cacti of the south. *Sagebrush*, mesquite, salt bush and prickly pear cactus are the main plants of the Great Basin.

The lowest point in the states is in the **Mojave Desert** (Mo ha' vay) in Death Valley National Monument. When you see *joshua trees* you know you are in the Mojave Desert.

The **Sonora Desert** is the one most people think of when desert is mentioned. This is where you find the stately *saguaro* (sa wah' row) and organ pipe cacti. Most of this desert is in Mexico but it extends north into Arizona and southern California.

Like the Sonoran Desert, the **Chihuahuan** (Chih wah' won) **Desert** is mostly in Mexico, but you can see the indicator *lechuguilla* (lay chew ghee' ah) plant and other agaves (ah gah' vay) in southern New Mexico and Texas.

The **Colorado Plateau** is Canyon Country. Here you will find colorful rocks and arches of many well known National Parks and Monuments like Grand Canyon, Canyonlands, Arches, and Monument Valley. Snow capped mountains rise from the plateau, and rivers have cut deep canyons through it. Yet it is dry country with rain and snow falling mostly on the mountains. Juniper and pinyon pine shade the higher slopes and cottonwood trees line the rivers.

sagebrush

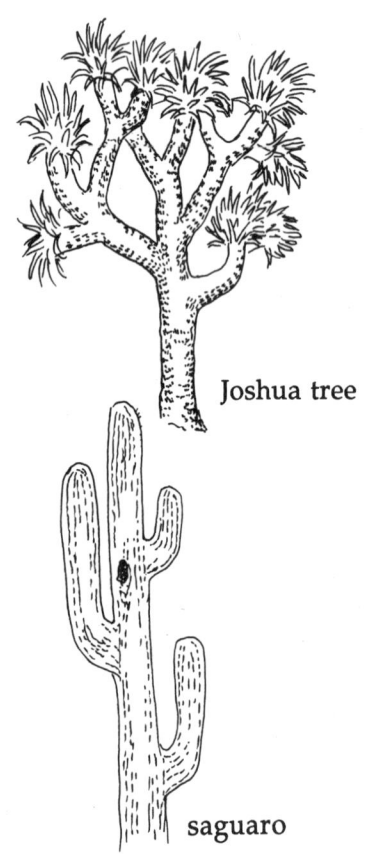

Joshua tree

saguaro

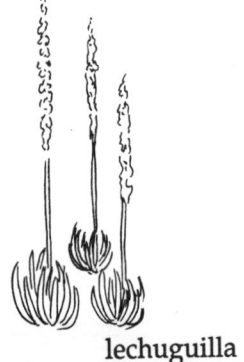

lechuguilla

Canyonlands National Park

4

Deserts and Canyons of the Southwest

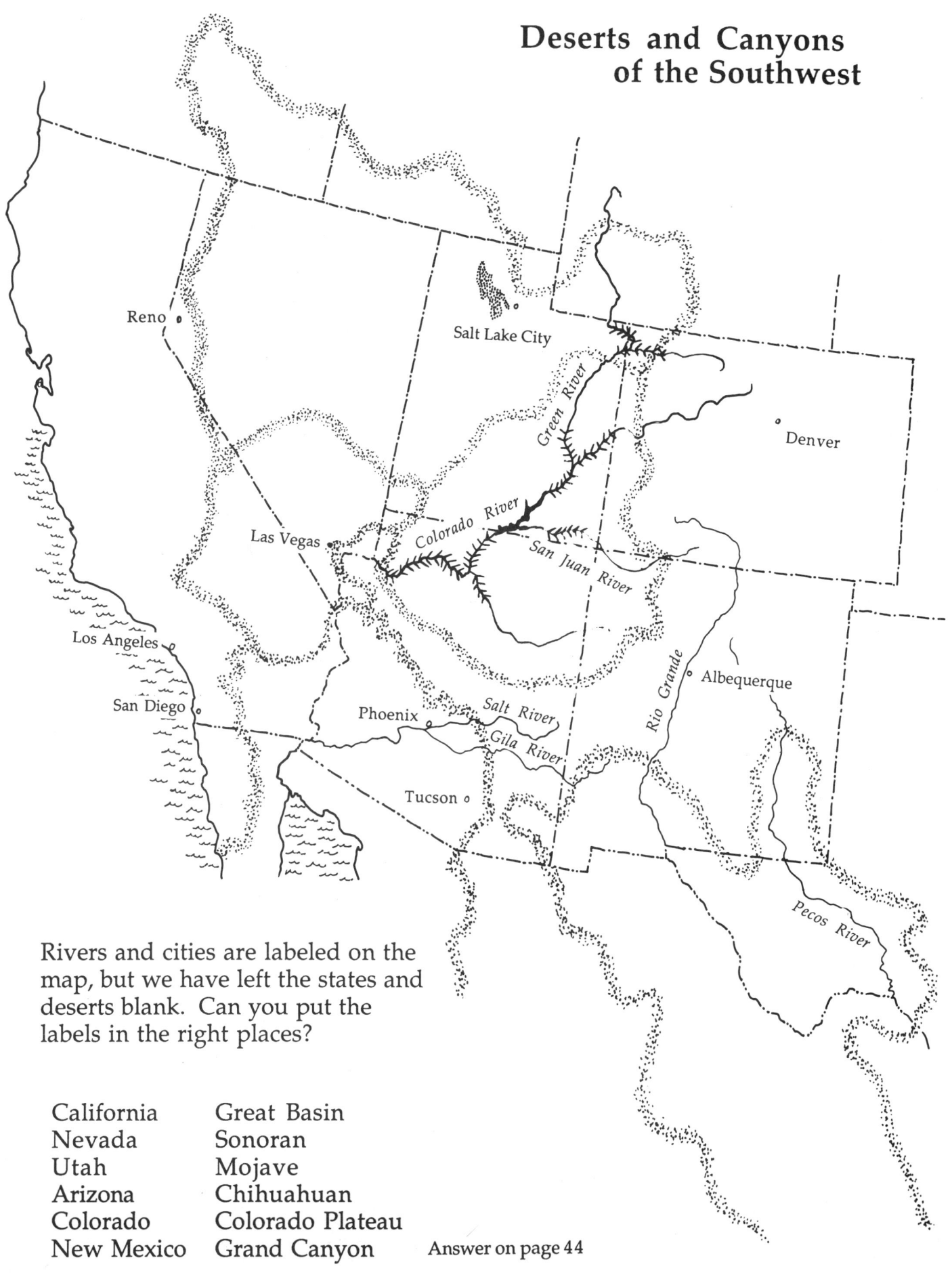

Reno

Salt Lake City

Green River

Denver

Colorado River

San Juan River

Las Vegas

Los Angeles

San Diego

Phoenix

Salt River

Gila River

Tucson

Rio Grande

Albequerque

Pecos River

Rivers and cities are labeled on the map, but we have left the states and deserts blank. Can you put the labels in the right places?

California	Great Basin
Nevada	Sonoran
Utah	Mojave
Arizona	Chihuahuan
Colorado	Colorado Plateau
New Mexico	Grand Canyon

Answer on page 44

Some Words to Know

CARRION—The flesh of animals already dead and starting to decay. Many animals feed on carrion, something killed by disease, accident, or by other animals.

CARNIVORES—Flesh-eating animals such as dogs, cats, bears, and hawks.

HABITAT—The land or space where a plant or animal lives. An animal's habitat needs to provide food, water, and shelter.

HIBERNATE—A deep, sound sleep during the winter months. An animal that hibernates usually will not wake up even if disturbed.

PREDATORS—Animals that kill others for food. Most carnivores are predators.

PREY—The animal or animals that are killed for food.

RODENTS—Mammals like mice, squirrels and beaver. Rodents' front teeth grow all their lives and need to be worn down by gnawing.

CANINE—Mammals of the dog family such as coyotes, wolves and foxes.

NOCTURNAL—Animals that are out and about hunting and feeding at night.

Wildlife Oasis

There are 40 birds and mammals hiding in the green oasis with its clear cool spring on the next page. Can you find them. If you can't recognize them all now, read through this book and you will know them better. Answer on page 45

antelope squirrel	cottontail	hummingbird	prairie dog
badger	coyote	jackrabbit	pronghorn
bat	dove	javalina	quail
bighorn	eagle	kangaroo rat	raccoon
black-troated sparrow	elf owl	kit fox	ringtail
bobcat	flicker	mountain lion	roadrunner
cactus wren	gila woodpecker	mouse	rock squirrel
cardinal	gnatcatcher	mule deer	skunk
chipmunk	great horned owl	pinyon jay	turkey vulture
coati	grey fox	porcupine	vermilion flycatcher

The **Gila woodpecker** (hee' la) makes its home in tall cactus country. Saguaro and organ pipe provide fine protection, food, and moisture. Stout chisel-like bills carve cozy holes in the cacti. **Elf owls** will often move in after a woodpecker has deserted a cavity. Dark **turkey vultures** have no feathers on their red heads. These carrion eaters use tall saguaros for lookout posts and often build nests in branches.

If the **collared lizard** outruns the **roadrunner**, the bird may catch a beetle or other insect, snake or small rodent. This speedy bird can run at over 15 miles per hour. It prefers to stay on the ground, but can fly when it wants. **Pinacate beetles** "stand on their heads" if they feel threatened. The lechuguilla plant is an indicator species for the Chihuahuan desert.

Sharp spines of cactus plants give protection to the nests of many desert birds like the **curve-billed thrasher** (top) and the **cactus wren.** The wren even weaves prickly spines around the tunnel-like opening of its nest. The flowers of the cane cholla are red. Those of the fuzzy-looking teddy bear cholla are yellow green. Both have yellow centers. You can tell the grey-brown thrasher by its red-orange eyes. The wren has a white line above the eyes on its red-brown head.

The bright red **cardinal** is often seen in the southwest and the east around gardens and brushy areas, but it is also found along streams and near ponds. A **Pyrrhuloxia** (pie ruh locks' ee uh) sits on an ocotillo branch with red flowers. They are like cardinals in shape, but they are not all red and have a curved parrot-like bill. They are found in dryer areas than cardinals. Both feed on seeds and insects.

Quail live in brushy areas of the desert near a permanent source of water.
Gamble's quail (bottom) and **scaled quail** (right) like lower slopes and canyons,
while the colorful **Montezuma quail** (top) likes the higher forested slopes. Even
though they are adapted to dry areas, they need water regularly. Family groups
feed together on seeds and fruit of the brushy plants they also use for shelter.

The **mourning dove** (on branch) is the most common dove. Look for it along roadsides, in fields, and on telephone wires and fences. The other doves are found mostly near rivers among cottonwood trees and willow thickets. The **white-winged dove** (top) can sometimes be seen feeding on cactus fruit. The smaller **Inca dove** and **ground dove** are most often seen on the ground hunting for seed.

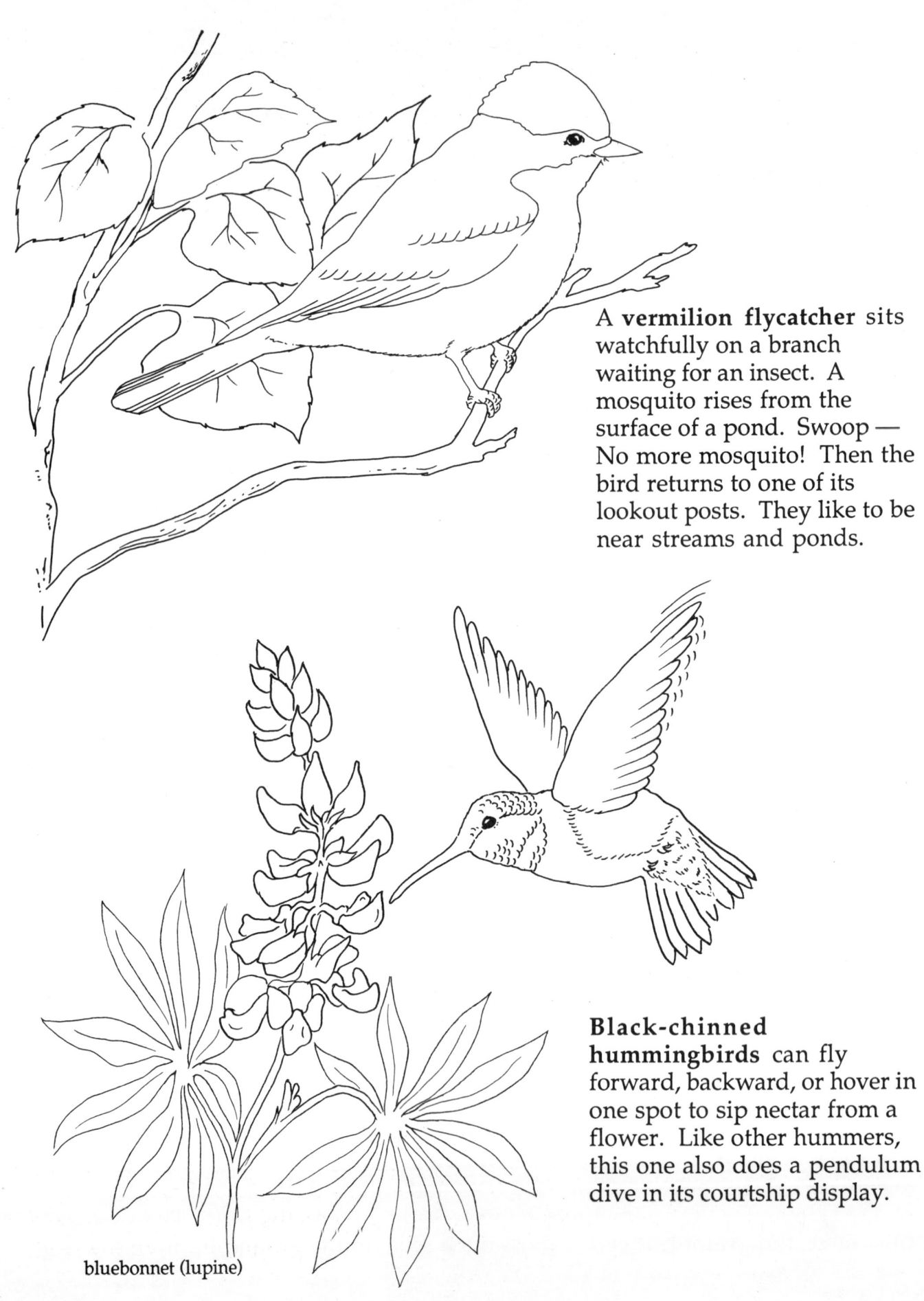

A **vermilion flycatcher** sits watchfully on a branch waiting for an insect. A mosquito rises from the surface of a pond. Swoop — No more mosquito! Then the bird returns to one of its lookout posts. They like to be near streams and ponds.

Black-chinned hummingbirds can fly forward, backward, or hover in one spot to sip nectar from a flower. Like other hummers, this one also does a pendulum dive in its courtship display.

bluebonnet (lupine)

Prickly Puzzle

Can you put all the words in the right places in the cholla plant puzzle? Remember only one letter in each square.

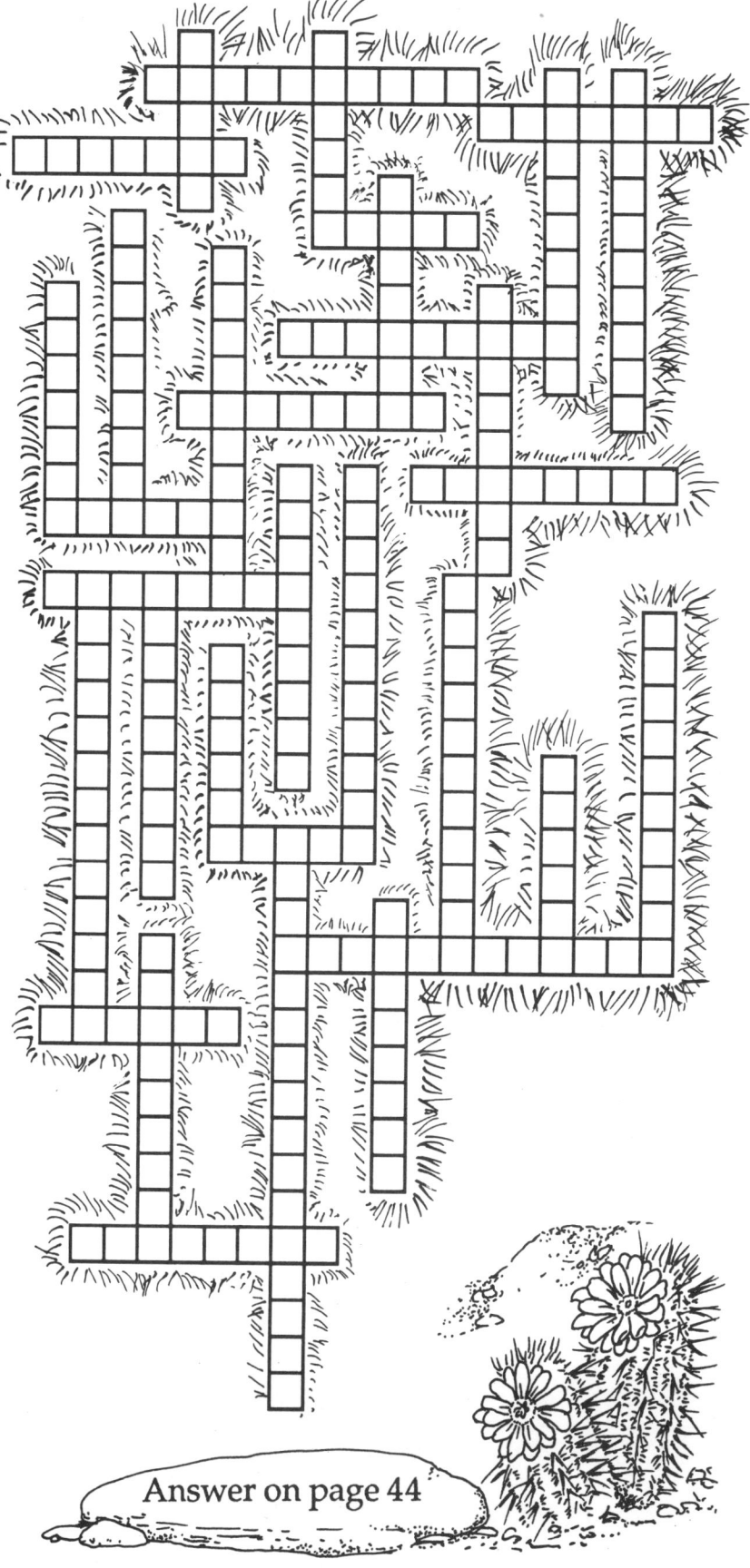

Answer on page 44

5 letter words
AGAVE
SOTOL
YUCCA

6 letter words
BANANA
BARREL
PENCIL
SENITA
TORREY

7 letter words
CHOLLAS
JUMPING
RAINBOW
SAGUARO

8 letter words
FISHHOOK
HEDGEHOG
IRONWOOD
MESQUITE
OCOTILLO
STAGHORN

9 letter words
CHRISTMAS
ORGAN PIPE
PALOVERDE
SCREWBEAN
SMOKETREE
TEDDYBEAR

10 letter words
BEAVERTAIL
CHAINFRUIT
JOSHUA TREE
PINCUSHION

11 letter words
LECHUGHILLA
PRICKLYPEAR

12 letter word
CENTURY PLANT

13 letter word
CATCLAW ACACIA

16 letter word
CRUCIFIXION THORN

A red, yellow, and black **western tanager** watches a family of mountain lions from the safety of a juniper tree. The **mountain lion** has many names — cougar, puma, panther. Like all cats, claws do not show in their tracks.

Deer, rabbits, and other small animals are their main food, though they will sometimes hunt bighorn and the young of larger animals.

A **bobcat** comes around an
ironwood tree and surprises a
badger. This chance
encounter will produce a lot of
hissing, growling, and snarling,
but in the end the shy badger will probably retreat underground. Both animals
prey mainly on rodents, but their methods are different. The bobcat stalks quietly
or waits hidden by a game trail to pounce upon its prey. The badger uses its
powerful feet and claws to dig out its meals.

17

A **flicker** pauses in a pinyon pine while a family of grey foxes watch. The **grey fox** is the only canine that can climb trees. Sometimes they even have their dens in hollow trees. They sneak up on their prey and strike in a catlike manner or they will lie in wait by a rabbit trail until the prey comes along. They are most active at night but are sometimes seen in the evening or early morning.

The **coyote** is an adaptable animal, and is found in most parts of the U.S. The vixen will make her den among rocks or under a log or sometimes she will enlarge the burrow of another animal. Coyotes hunt rabbits and mice, but also feed on some plants and insects. The joshua tree has long narrow leaves and clusters of creamy white blossoms.

hedgehog cactus

Don't be surprised to find the eyes of a small cat-sized animal watching you from the shadows around your campfire. The sandy-colored **kit fox** is very curious and looks for all sorts of things as he wanders about at night. **Kangaroo mice**, rats, and other rodents are the main food, but they also eat insects, lizards, and snakes. Their large ears are lined with long hairs to keep desert sand out.

There are four kinds of skunks in the southwest. All are usually nocturnal, hunting at night for insects, lizards, mice, eggs, berries, and roots. The **striped skunk** is the most common. If you are lucky you may see a parade of mother and kits looking for food around dusk.

The **hognosed skunk** uses its tough bare snout to root out insects.

The small **spotted skunk** can climb trees. When you see a handstand like this —beware!

The **hooded skunk** has a ruff of long fur at the neck and a very long tail.

A **mule deer** buck in velvet surprises a doe and fawn in a brushy thicket. Bucks lose their antlers in winter and start growing a new set every spring. While antlers are growing they have a soft velvety covering. A young fawn has no odor to attract predators, and will lie very still in brush for up to three hours. The doe may wander off to lead predators away. She will return when danger is past.

Desert bighorn are now found in only a few remote or protected places. They can go without water for several days. Lambs are born in the spring and stay with the ewes for the first year. Only the rams have large curling horns, and they stay in groups by themselves most of the year. A shiny black raven perches in a bristlecone pine to survey the landscape for carrion.

pincushion cactus

The fastest mammal in North America, **Pronghorn** can run more than 50 miles an hour for short distances. Even the light brown kids can outrun a coyote by the time they are two weeks old. The outer part of the horn is shed every year. Large eyes can spot the slightest movement as much as three miles away. Prairie dogs and burrowing owls share the open land that pronghorn prefer. **Burrowing owls** are quick to retreat to their holes when frightened.

Tracks! Tracks! Tracks!

BOBCAT___ COTTONTAIL___ COYOTE___
LIZARD___ MULE DEER___ QUAIL___ RACCOON___
ROADRUNNER___ SIDEWINDER ___ KANGAROO RAT___

In hot dry country don't expect to see lots of wildlife during the day. Darkness gives protection and at night precious moisture is not lost to heat and dry winds. But look closely during the day. Signs can tell stories about things that happened earlier. Can you match these animals with their tracks? (Place a number in the space after each name.) Then for an extra challenge *tell what happened* in each of the five sets. Answer on page 44

Collared **peccary** or "**javalina**" will eat prickly pear cactus, spines and all, mesquite beans and other fruits and plants. You are most likely to see them early in the morning or at night. They travel in family groups of as many as 30 or 40. The young javalinas are reddish brown when small, but turn grey as they grow. The **chuckwalla**, a large brown lizard, also feeds on cactus and other succulent desert plants. When frightened he will crawl into a crack in the rocks and swell his body so he can't be pulled out.

willow   yellow columbine

The black and orange **oriole** has a white wing patch. It watches a **raccoon** family hunting for food. Raccoons are never found very far from water, so you are more likely to see them in canyons or along rivers. They will eat just about anything — insects, eggs, small animals, fruit, and fish.

Shiny black **phainopeplas** (fay no pep' la) scold as a curious **coati** (co ah' tee) investigates a nest in a paloverde tree. Coatis hunt and travel in groups of a few to as many as 30 or more. The long sensitive nose and claws are used in rooting out food such as scorpions and other insects, small mammals, and snakes. Coatis will eat just about anything they can find. The black mask and lightly striped tail show they are related to the raccoon.

A **ringtail** moves quietly among the branches of a desert live oak. It has large eyes so it can see well at night. It is sometimes called a miner's cat because miners kept them around to kill mice and rats. They also eat lizard, insects and eggs. The desert **woodrat** builds a large nest of sticks, grass, cactus, and odd pieces of junk he finds.

A **porcupine**'s love of salt makes old boots, tires and fence posts targets for gnawing. Their main food is the bark of trees, plants and twigs. A new born porcupine has soft quills, but they harden quickly. Young are able to climb trees and eat plants within a few hours of birth. The blue-gray **pinyon jay** has nothing to fear from this strict vegetarian as long as it keeps a safe distance.

A diving hawk with talons extended can terrify a whole colony of **prairie dogs**. This **red-tailed hawk** would like to make a meal of a prairie dog. It will have to be fast to catch one before they all disappear into their holes. One gives a warning whistle and they all dive for shelter. The mounds of earth around the entrances shed water and serve as raised lookouts for danger.

gold poppy

The **desert cottontail** makes a den in a burrow, or in a mesquite or catclaw acacia thicket. There the thorny bushes keep many predators away. **Gnatcatchers** often flit among the branches of these thickets, too. They are shy, gray and black birds. The best time to look for them is in the morning or evening.

A **golden eagle** flies into open country in search of food, perhaps an unwary rabbit. The **black-tailed jackrabbit** (really a hare) can outrun almost any predator. Large ears can detect the faintest sound, and the bulging eyes give a wide range of vision. The **antelope jackrabbit** is very much like the black-tailed but doesn't have the black on tail or tips of ears. Antelope jackrabbits tend to wait motionless but watchful until the last minute before fleeing with great bounds of 15 to 20 feet.

rabbit brush

staghorn cholla

elephant tree

The little **antelope ground squirrel** looks much like a chipmunk, but the stripes end at the shoulder instead of the tip of the nose. Friendly and playful, they are fond of seeds and fruit of all kinds. Cactus spines do not keep them from scurrying up to feed on juicy fruit pods. The **black-throated sparrow** has a grey back and white breast around a black bib. It also feeds on seeds and fruit of desert plants.

34

Rocky canyons are the place to look for **rock squirrels** and cliff **chipmunks**. The rock squirrel is hard to see because his gray coat blends in so well with the rocks. Chipmunks scurry among boulders, brush, and low trees in search of seed and nuts. Notice the stripes on the face of the chipmunk.

A **kangaroo rat**, cheeks stuffed with seeds, is chased away by another. In the tussle over a cache of seeds, they are not aware of danger from the sky. Like the **great horned owl**, kangaroo rats are out only at night and even shun a bright moon. Large eyes and sensitive ears and the ability to leap 10 feet or more is the rat's defense against many night predators. They can live their whole life without a drink of water. The light yellow flowers of the **organ pipe cactus** also bloom at night.

Bats are the only mammals that can truly fly. They maneuver in the dark by means of echolocation, their natural sonar. High-pitched sounds are sent out and reflected back to sensitive ears if an object is in the area. The **Mexican freetail bat** shown here lives in large colonies in caves. They will fly up to a hundred miles a night in search of insects. In winter they migrate south.

Lizards

Lizards are cold-blooded animals. Most of them need to bask in the sun to warm up before they can move about very fast. Still they usually do not like the hottest part of the day. Some of them are active only at night. Food is usually insects and spiders, but some will feed on other lizards and small rodents.

Don't be confused by the funny looking names. The letters have been scrambled in each name. Your challenge is to unscramble them. See inside of back cover for help.

Answer on page 44

1. GRIFEN-DOTE DILRAZ
The fringe on his toes helps him run swiftly through sand.

2. RAZEB LEDITA RIDLAZ
Also named for its tail, this speedy runner will eat anything it can catch

3. TREEDS ANIGUA
This one likes it really hot (115° or more) and goes into rodent burrows.

4. DIES CHETOBLED ZILRAD
This common lizard has dark blue or black blotches on its sides.

5. THAWPILI
This one is named for the long slender tail that is bright blue in young ones.

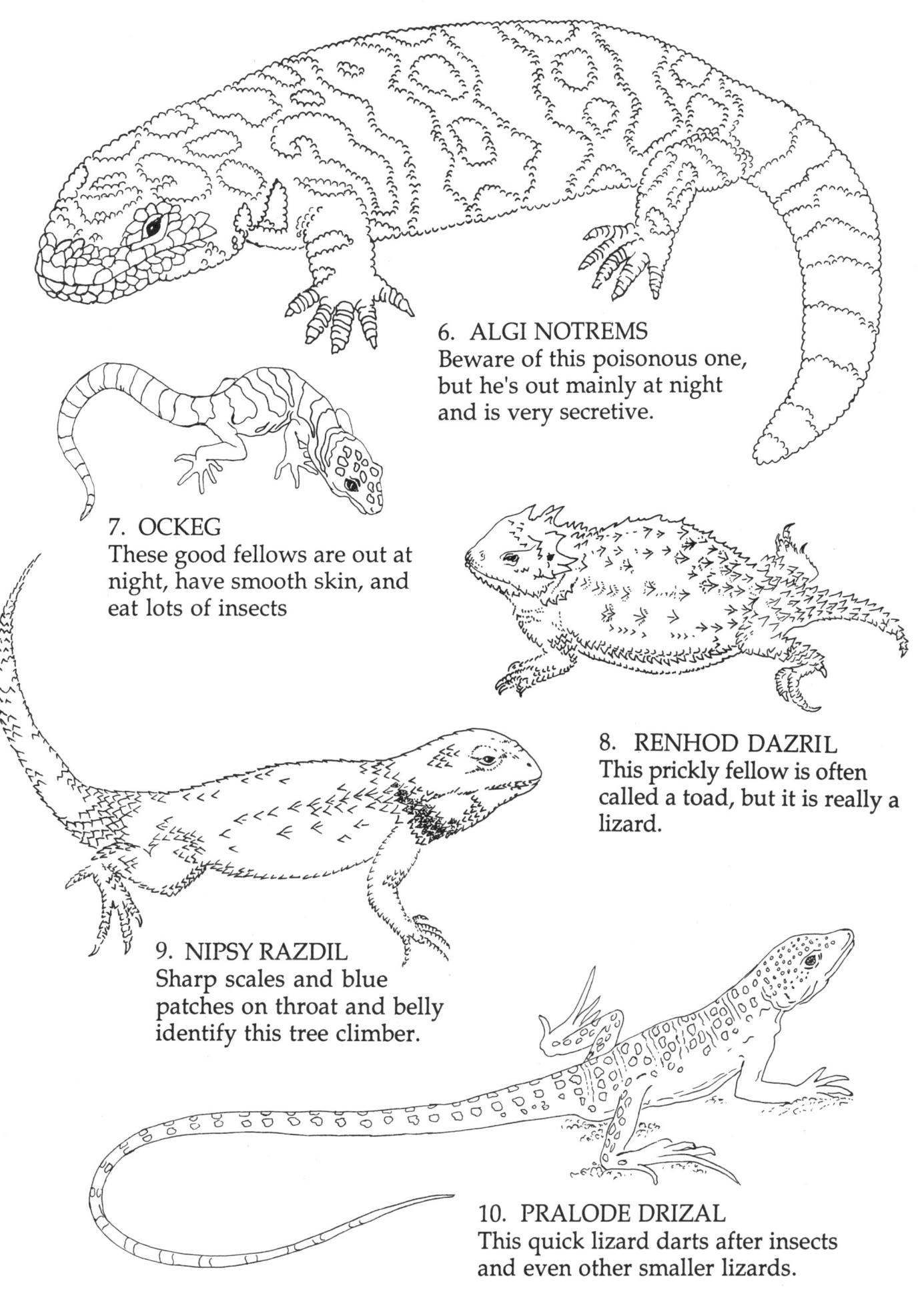

6. ALGI NOTREMS
Beware of this poisonous one, but he's out mainly at night and is very secretive.

7. OCKEG
These good fellows are out at night, have smooth skin, and eat lots of insects

8. RENHOD DAZRIL
This prickly fellow is often called a toad, but it is really a lizard.

9. NIPSY RAZDIL
Sharp scales and blue patches on throat and belly identify this tree climber.

10. PRALODE DRIZAL
This quick lizard darts after insects and even other smaller lizards.

Desert Puzzles

This creature digs a long deep burrow for shelter when it is very hot or cold. It gets all the moisture it needs from green vegetation it eats. For some reason they do not live in captivity and do not like to be handled. To find out who it is, connect the two sets of dots in numerical or alphabetical order.

Answer on page 44

Several creatures are hiding in the foliage in this picture. To find them, use the following key to color the different sections:

1. green   2. yellow   3. tan   4. black   5. brown   6. orange

You will find the answer and more information about them on page 45.

STINGERS AND BITERS

There is no need to fear spiders, insects and snakes that bite, but you do need to be careful. In fact you will be lucky to see most of these animals. The few that are dangerously poisonous are very secretive, or out only at night, or both. However it is a good idea to know a little about them.

Insects and spiders

Velvet ants are really wingless wasps. They scurry along the ground like ants and pack a painful sting. **Centipedes** have only one leg on each body segment. It has a painful bite but is not dangerous. They feed on other insects.
Tarantulas are furry dangerous looking spiders. They can sting but the venom is no stronger than that of a bee. They live in web lined holes in the ground and are out hunting insects at night.
Scorpions come in different colors and shapes. Some are <u>quite poisonous</u>. The females carry young on their backs until they can defend themselves.

Poisonous Snakes

Rattlesnakes are pit vipers. They have a temperature sensitive pit between the nose and eye. The long hollow fangs fold back against the roof of the mouth when closed. Rattlesnakes come in many colors and sizes, but they all have shell like segments at the end of the tail that make a buzzing sound when the snake is alarmed. Several rattlesnakes are shown in the maze on the next page. The sidewinder has horns over each eye and moves quickly over sand with a sideways motion, making an unusual pattern.

The **Arizona coral snake** has many look alikes. None are exactly the same. The banded **sand snake** has black and yellow bands bands around the body but no bright red. Next is the poisonous **coral snake** with alternating red and black bands separated by yellow all around the body. The **shovelnos snake** has the same color pattern but the bands do not circle the body. The same is true of the larger **longnosed snake** and there are white flecks in the red and black sections. **Arizona mountain king snakes** are larger than coral snakes and have red and light yellow bands separated by black

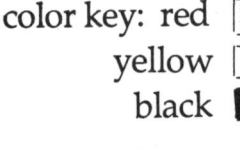

color key: red
yellow
black

SNAKE MAZE

Here are lots of snakes: snakes with bands like the coral, shovelnose, longnosed, and sand snake; snakes with stripes like the rosy boa, striped whipsnake, patchnose, and garter snakes; snakes with blotches like rattlesnakes, glossy, gopher, king, and lyre snakes. Can you make your way through this maze without getting bitten by a poisonous snake? (See page 42 and inside front cover for descriptions.) You can go by the tail of any snake, but watch out for the fangs and heads of the poisonous ones. There are several snakes that have red, black, and yellow patterns. <u>Only one of these is poisonous.</u> You may want to color them first. Below is a list of the snakes in this maze. A • indicates a poisonous snake, and numbers in ( ) show how many there are.

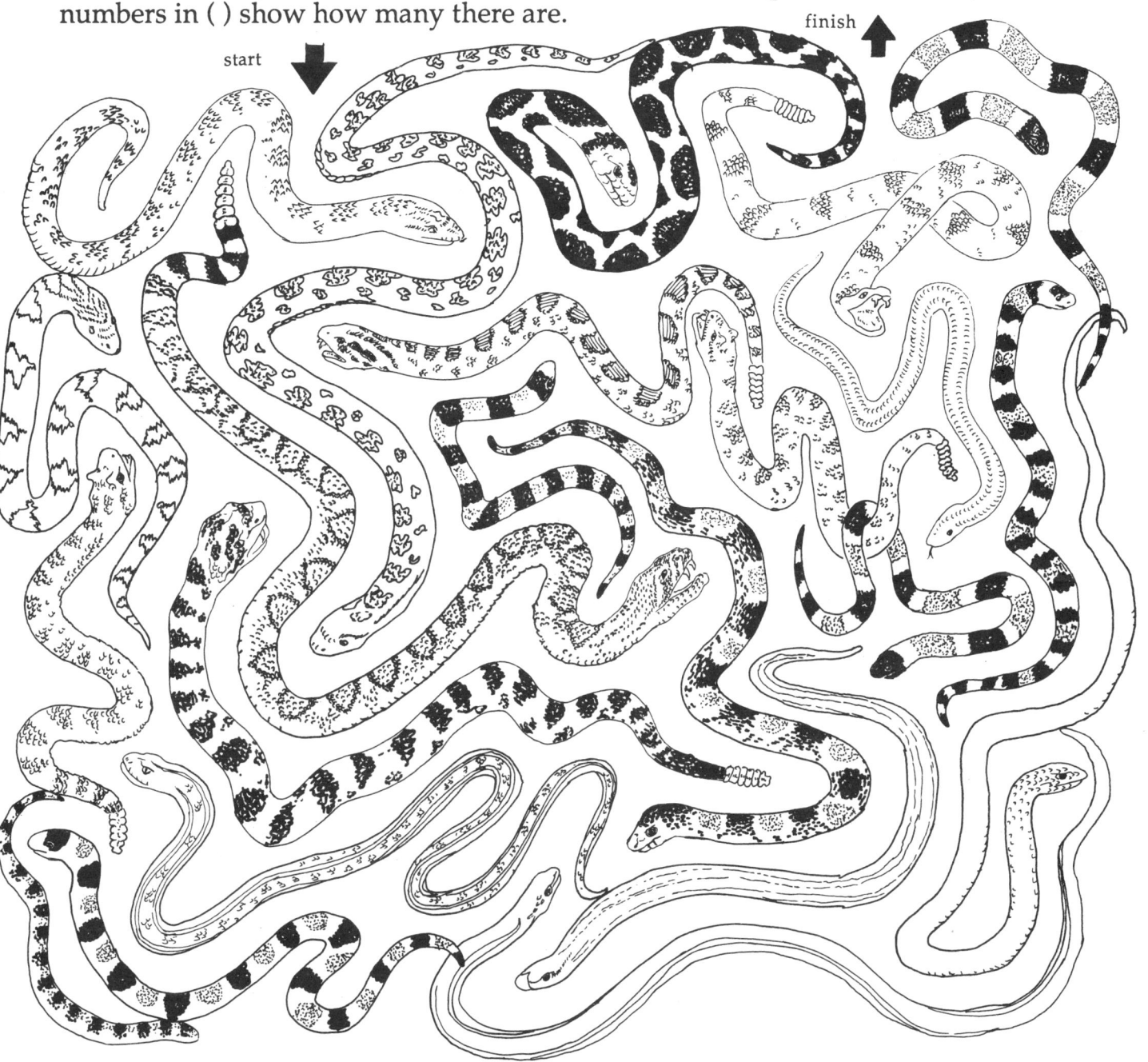

COMMON KINGSNAKE   CORAL SNAKE •(2)   GARTER SNAKE   GLOSSY
SNAKE GOPHER SNAKE   LONGNOSE SNAKE   LYRE SNAKE
MASSASAUGA •   PATCHNOSE SNAKE RACER   RATTLESNAKE •(3)
ROSY BOA   SAND SNAKE   SHOVELNOSE SNAKE   SIDEWINDER •(2)
STRIPED WHIPSNAKE   MOUNTAIN KING SNAKE

Answer on page 45

Deserts and Canyons of the Southwest

Page 5 **Map**

Page 15 **Prickly puzzle**

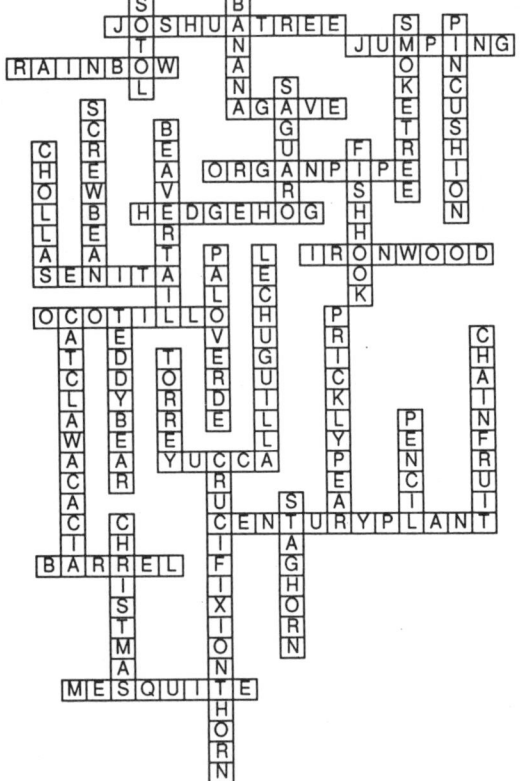

Page 38 **Lizards**

1. FRINGE-TOED LIZARD
2. ZEBRA TAILED LIZARD
3. DESERT IGUANA
4. SIDE BLOTCHED
5. WHIPTAIL
6. GILA MONSTER
7. GECKO
8. HORNED LIZARD
9. SPINY LIZARD
10. LEOPARD LIZARD

Page 40 **Desert Puzzle**

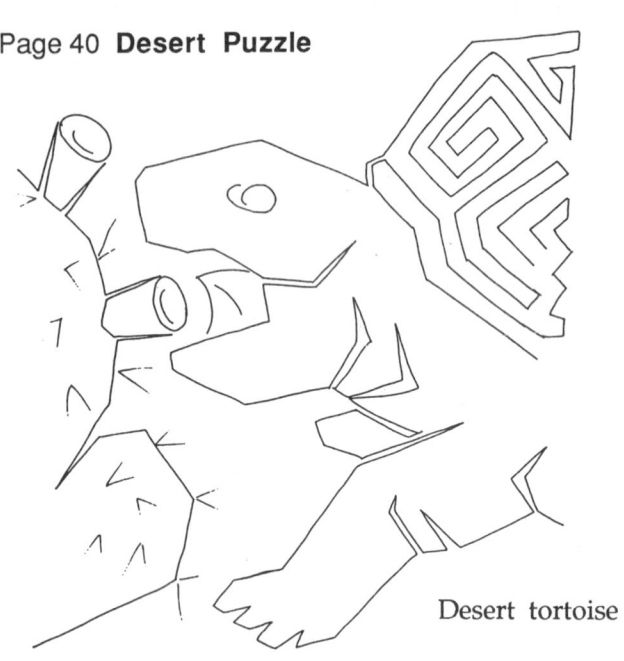

Desert tortoise

Page 25 **Tracks**

Set 1. A sidewinder follows a kangaroo rat into its nesting hol

Set 2. A roadrunner spots a collared lizard and chases it.

Set 3. A coyote comes across the tracks of a quail and follows i until it flies.

Set 4. A bobcat sees a cottontail and chases it.

Set 5. Raccoon and deer tracks at a desert water hole.

BOBCAT _4a_ COTTONTAIL _4b_ COYOTE _3b_
LIZARD _2b_ MULE DEER _5b_ QUAIL _3a_ RACCOON _5a_
ROADRUNNER _2a_ SIDEWINDER _1a_ KANGAROO RAT _1b

Page 46 **Wordsearch**

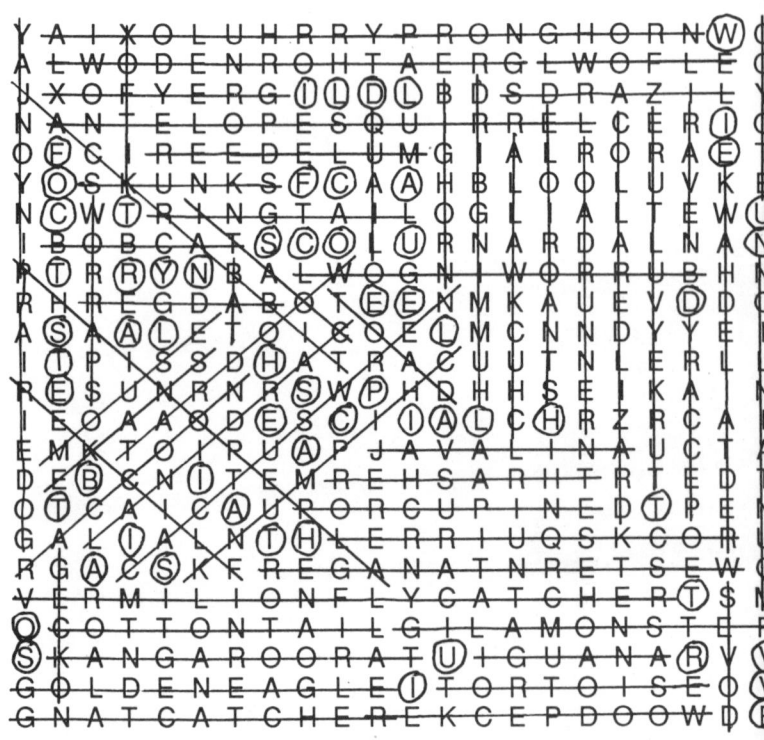

Wildlife of cactus country needs all the special habitat it has to survive.

Pinacate beetles are sometimes called circus beetles from their habit of standing on their heads when threatened.
Millipedes have two legs on most body segments. Though they are usually under ground, they are often seen after rain.
Grasshoppers grow up to three inches long. They are plant eaters and in turn provide food for many desert animals.
Spadefoot toads have an interesting life cycle, spending most of it under ground. After a rain they emerge, breed and the young are full grown in a few weeks, before the moisture is gone.
Tarantula hawks sting and bury tarantulas. An egg is layed with the spider, and the larva feed on it. They are colorful black and orange insects.

Page 3
Learning to Survive

```
 1        W A X Y
 2          D O R M A N T
 3        H A I R
 4        S P I N E S
 5    R O O T S
 6      L E A V E S
 7        S T O R E
 8    R A D I A T I N G
 9      F O O D
10        N O C T U R N A L
11        S L E E P
```

Page 43 **Snake Maze**

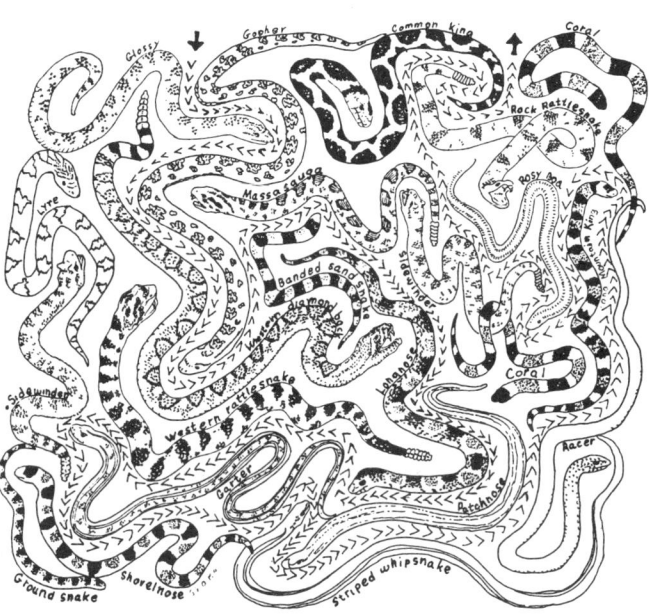

Page 7 **Wildlife Oasis**

1	antelope squirrel	21	hummingbird
2	badger	22	jackrabbit
3	bat	23	javalina
4	bighorn	24	kangaroo rat
5	black-troated sparrow	25	kit fox
6	bobcat	26	mountain lion
7	cactus wren	27	mouse
8	cardinal	28	mule deer
9	chipmunk	29	pinyon jay
10	coati	30	porcupine
11	cottontail	31	prairie dog
12	coyote	32	pronghorn
13	dove	33	quail
14	eagle	34	raccoon
15	elf owl	35	ringtail
16	flicker	36	roadrunner
17	gila woodpecker	37	rock squirrel
18	gnatcatcher	38	skunk
19	great horned owl	39	turkey vulture
20	grey fox	40	vermilion flycatcher

Wildlife Wordsearch

All the animals and reptiles in this book are hidden in the block of letters. Use the words from the list of animals in the index on page 47 as your guide to find all the words. When you have crossed off all the animals the letters that are left will spell a sentence. Write them in order on the spaces below to discover what it is.

Answer on page 44

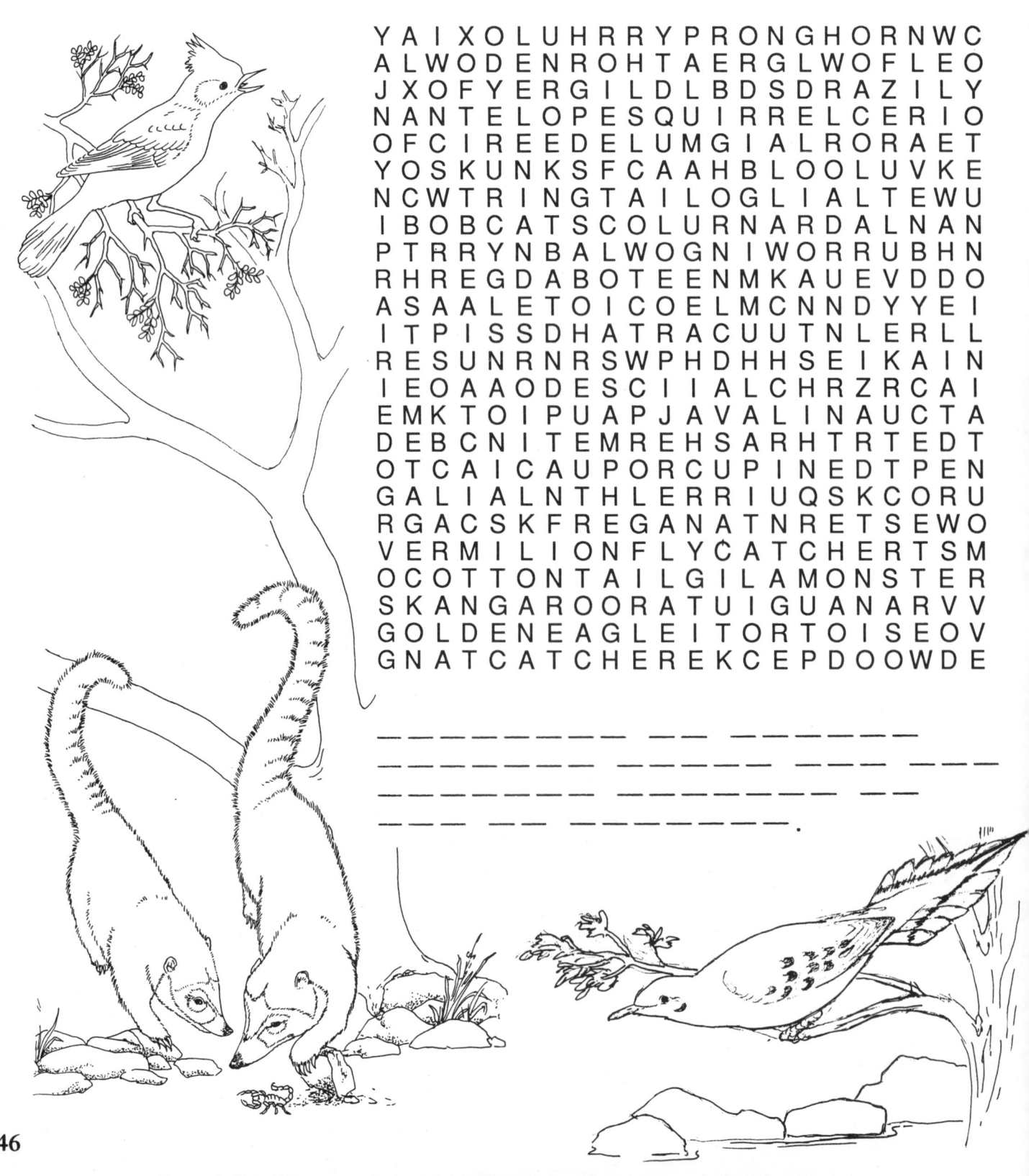

```
Y A I X O L U H R R Y P R O N G H O R N W C
A L W O D E N R O H T A E R G L W O F L E O
J X O F Y E R G I L D L B D S D R A Z I L Y
N A N T E L O P E S Q U I R R E L C E R I O
O F C I R E E D E L U M G I A L R O R A E T
Y O S K U N K S F C A A H B L O O L U V K E
N C W T R I N G T A I L O G L I A L T E W U
I B O B C A T S C O L U R N A R D A L N A N
P T R R Y N B A L W O G N I W O R R U B H N
R H R E G D A B O T E E N M K A U E V D D O
A S A A L E T O I C O E L M C N N D Y Y E I
I T P I S S D H A T R A C U U T N L E R L L
R E S U N R N R S W P H D H H S E I K A I N
I E O A A O D E S C I I A L C H R Z R C A I
E M K T O I P U A P J A V A L I N A U C T A
D E B C N I T E M R E H S A R H T R T E D T
O T C A I C A U P O R C U P I N E D T P E N
G A L I A L N T H L E R R I U Q S K C O R U
R G A C S K F R E G A N A T N R E T S E W O
V E R M I L I O N F L Y C A T C H E R T S M
O C O T T O N T A I L G I L A M O N S T E R
S K A N G A R O O R A T U I G U A N A R V V
G O L D E N E A G L E I T O R T O I S E O V
G N A T C A T C H E R E K C E P D O O W D E
```

_ _ _ _ _ _ _ _ _   _ _   _ _ _ _ _ _

_ _ _ _ _ _ _   _ _ _   _ _ _ _ _   _ _ _

_ _ _ _   _ _ _ _ _ _ _ _   _ _

_ _ _   _ _   _ _ _ _ _ _ _ .

INDEX OF ANIMALS AND WORDSEARCH WORDS

Use the extra columns for the wordsearch and for a checklist of plants and animals you see.

yucca

INDEX OF PLANTS

YOUR PAGE

Use this page to draw a picture, keep a journal of your trip, or make notes.